YOUR KNOWLEDGE HAS VALUE

- We will publish your bachelor's and master's thesis, essays and papers

- Your own eBook and book - sold worldwide in all relevant shops

- Earn money with each sale

Upload your text at www.GRIN.com and publish for free

Bibliographic information published by the German National Library:

The German National Library lists this publication in the National Bibliography; detailed bibliographic data are available on the Internet at http://dnb.dnb.de .

This book is copyright material and must not be copied, reproduced, transferred, distributed, leased, licensed or publicly performed or used in any way except as specifically permitted in writing by the publishers, as allowed under the terms and conditions under which it was purchased or as strictly permitted by applicable copyright law. Any unauthorized distribution or use of this text may be a direct infringement of the author s and publisher s rights and those responsible may be liable in law accordingly.

Imprint:

Copyright © 2006 GRIN Verlag, Open Publishing GmbH
Print and binding: Books on Demand GmbH, Norderstedt Germany
ISBN: 9783668368743

This book at GRIN:

http://www.grin.com/en/e-book/110867/the-cult-of-citizenship-education-by-a-sears-and-e-hyslop-margison-a

Michael Ernest Sweet

The Cult of Citizenship Education by A. Sears and E. Hyslop-Margison. A Review

GRIN Publishing

GRIN - Your knowledge has value

Since its foundation in 1998, GRIN has specialized in publishing academic texts by students, college teachers and other academics as e-book and printed book. The website www.grin.com is an ideal platform for presenting term papers, final papers, scientific essays, dissertations and specialist books.

Visit us on the internet:

http://www.grin.com/

http://www.facebook.com/grincom

http://www.twitter.com/grin_com

The Cult of Citizenship Education

Reviewed by Michael Ernest Sweet

Concordia University Montreal

September 18, 2006

The Cult of Citizenship Education

"A dread that goes beyond the breakdown of bowling leagues and civic clubs... the fear of our young as letterless, unassailable barbarians"
(Pinsky, 2002).

Alan Sears and Emery Hyslop-Margison, in *The Cult of Citizenship Education*, illuminate the driving discourse behind the seeming explosion in democratic citizenship education reform with particular attention to the last decade.

Sears and Hyslop-Margison lay a solid foundation of scholarship to support their claim of a climate of educational reform driven by mere slogans and dogma, rather than any meaningful research or reliable data. Calling on Janice Gross Stein's 2001 Massey Lectures, *The Cult of Efficiency*, Sears and Hyslop-Margison, in accessible terms, explain that meaningful dialogue around issues of educational reform is precluded by the participants being caught up in a maze of rapid-fire rhetoric. As a result, *The Cult of Citizenship Education*, is a call for a more careful, thoughtful, and nuanced approach in understanding and promoting democratic citizenship education and its reform.

Moving forward, Sears and Hyslop-Margison begin to analyze some of the rhetoric produced by this cult mentality. Their overarching claim is that a grossly distorted discourse of crisis has formed around the subject of citizenship education, and is a driving force in sweeping reforms resulting in little to no value in regards to meaningful reform. Sears and Hyslop-Margison synthesize the discourse of crisis into three main areas (1) the crisis of ignorance, (2) the crisis of alienation, and (3) the crisis of agnosticism. Calling forward a host of reputable scholars and research they attempt to disassemble these claims. Without wishing to compromise the integrity of their arguments, I will further summarize them for our purposes here.

Within the crisis of ignorance Sears and Hyslop-Margison assert that our youth are no more ignorant than that of a hundred years ago, and that which they are ignorant of is 'questionable' in its relevance to meaningful democratic citizenship; the listing of prime ministers and naming of famous Canadians was cited among other "arcane historical and political facts" (p. 18). Although respecting the potential problems associated with these perceived areas of ignorance in the Canadian population, Sears and Hyslop-Margison dismiss this as a crisis of citizenship stating that this knowledge is "not particularly essential to good citizenship" (p. 18).

Turning to the crisis of alienation, the authors refer to a conclusion of alienation from the socio-political apparatus that has been drawn, primarily, from steadily declining voter participation rates, especially among younger voters. Sears and Hyslop-Margison in essence endeavor to sever the idea of political alienation from that of civic alienation. Pointing to research that suggests contemporary youth are no more cynical than their parents, but rather less allegiant to partisan politics, concluding that today's youth are merely alienated from a "political system closed to meaningful consultation and participation" (Buckingham, 1999, as cited on p. 18). They proceed to illustrate that this does not translate into across-the-board civic disengagement, but does perhaps reflect the significant voter decline. In fact, the authors turn to Gautier (2002) to demonstrate that youth are turning to a form of participatory democracy; they are engaging in social movements such as environmentalism, and that this form of civic engagement is increasing. Thus, our youth have merely shifted their participation away from the purely political process to a more "grass roots" form of engagement.

Finally, in respect to the crisis of agnosticism, Sears and Hyslop-Margison argue that we cannot conclude, from such incidents as "ethically motivated attacks on foreign residents in Canada, Europe, and the United States" a "serious deficit of democratic values" (p. 20). Arguing that the situation is not this simple, the authors defer to a host of studies that have identified youth as "positive" towards an expanse of democratic values. In fact, they point to the willingness of youth to limit rights such as freedom of speech for groups promoting racism. Recognizing that some may see this denial of access as a low level commitment to fundamental democratic values, Sears and Hyslop-Margison respond by saying that it does demonstrate that young people are "genuinely concerned with ethno-cultural diversity" (p. 20). They end simply with a statement that the crisis of agnosticism is complex.

In their general conclusion to the article authors Alan Sears and Emery Hyslop-Margison reassert that there is a need to move from cult mentality (sweeping and unfounded generalizations, slogans and rhetoric) to a critical and reliable analysis of citizenship education reform. The problems arise when we begin to understand the *ipso facto* landscape of citizenship they have created in illustrating this point. In attempting to make a case for a careful, nuanced, and holistic analysis of citizenship education, the authors have actually proven the ease with which academic discourse can gloss over the very complexities they endeavored to highlight.

In their response to the crisis of ignorance, the authors do not consider the degree to which our youth understand, or do not understand, contemporary socio-political issues. I would assert that there is indeed a crisis of ignorance in this area. Political and historical facts are crucial "nuts and bolts" in the forming of complex understandings of contemporary issues. Further, there is much evidence to support the idea that the knowledge young people do have is disconnected from meaningful contexts. They are without a fundamental foundation of liberal education which allows a synchronization of knowledge to arrive at authentic understandings of complex situations. (see, for example, Hyslop-Margison, 2005). This becomes crucial when we turn to their arguments regarding the crisis of alienation. How might today's youth make a serious and meaningful impact by way of various social movements, such as environmentalism as the authors allude to, if they are without a genuine understanding of the fundamental nature at the heart of the problem? Further, how effective can any form of protest be without any meaningful connection to, or understanding of, the apparatus of governance which, ultimately, will need to be involved in substantial change to something like the environment which is essentially political? (see, for instance, Orr., 2004) To use the words of Sears and Hyslop-Margison there must be a balance with "the dispositional requirements of meaningful political engagement" and not simply a passing awareness of its function (p. 16). In effect, alienated from a political system, regardless of its nature or effectiveness, these youth are merely preaching to the converted- a general populace who, if also alienated from the political structure, are powerless to evoke any form of substantial change on a systemic level. Additionally, the authors leave us with a sense of the problem being exclusively that of the political structure and quote Osborne (2000) who in effect states that the problem rests with the political system and that the change is needed there and cannot be effected through better citizenship education.

This seems rather incongruous with fundamental concept of citizenship education. Is the idea not to change societal institutions, such as those which form 'government', by way of a more effective citizenry? Is change not effected by humans and are all humans not first and foremost citizens?

Within the crisis of agnosticism authors Sears and Hyslop-Margison again reduce the issue to a form of black and white in many respects. In response to a claim that our youth lack commitment to democratic virtues the authors provide research tantamount to a mere enumeration of democratic values knowledge among the youth population. The essential aspect they neglect is that identification of, or even an abstract understanding of democratic values does not equate to a "genuine" embodiment of the democratic spirit. I would refer to a quote provided by the authors elsewhere in the article which states that "don't teach us about the forms of democracy, we know all about the forms of democracy, we need to learn the spirit of democracy" (Herman, 1996, as quoted on p. 17). In fact, one might defer here to the work of these authors throughout their academic careers which have essentially established that our schools are teaching decontextualized democratic values (see, for example, Sears and Hughes, 1996; Hyslop-Margison and Graham, 2001; Hyslop-Margison, 2005). Thus, it should come as no surprise that our youth can reiterate them on survey upon survey. Being asked a question on a survey best resembles a test question whereby students are asked to reiterate information. Of course, they will supply an answer that is accepting and open towards immigrants, for instance, if that is what they have memorized, but this in no way equates to an evaluation of their "attitudes" which are truly manifest. Although I agree that the participants presenting a conflict in their support or free speech versus its actual application does not equate to a lack of commitment, I would suggest that it establishes their lack of internalization, and does not translate to a "genuine concern" as the authors would suggest.

In the end, the authors do not dismiss concern with the discourse of agnosticism, but they have given support to the idea that our youth are genuinely concerned with democratic values beyond that which we give them credit. The problem is that this assumption is based on information that simply reflects their awareness of the values and not their embodiment of such.

Although I give credit to the authors for hinting towards this dilemma throughout the article, I am disappointed that it did not figure into the discussion on agnosticism more deliberately. This is the very seat of the crisis in democratic citizenship.

Alan Sears and Emery Hyslop-Margison do succeed in forwarding a solid case for the need to take a much more nuanced, careful, and holistic look at democratic citizenship education reform. However, there is a sense of calm and "all-right-ness" emanating from this work that I would suggest is gravely dangerous. In over-simplifying the discourse of crises the authors have dismissed with the urgency rather than making it more exacting. Although, much of the "discourse of crisis" surrounding democratic citizenship and citizenship education may be off the mark, as they have established in many instances, this should not translate to an underestimation of the degree of urgency surrounding the problematics of genuine democratic engagement and civic virtue in contemporary youth. We do need to dispense with the cult mentality and its slogans and rhetoric, but in doing so we cannot afford to diminish the sense of crisis.

Perhaps the events of September 13, 2006 at Dawson College in Montreal where a young man opened fire on innocent, random students, gives substance to this disconnect between being theoretically aware of versus truly embodying human virtue. The various desirable dispositions of democratic citizenship, such as acceptance of diversity, can only truly manifest when experienced in relations to others. This connection between humans, as a virtue building exercise, is crucial. Contemporary democracy and capitalist economies have greatly diminished this by encouraging individual isolation and as a result young Canadians may "know" democratic virtues, but do not embody them in their very essence. It is this absence of *praxis* that should concern us with great urgency; concern us with a sense of crisis.

References

Hyslop-Margison, E. J. (2005). *Liberalizing vocational study: Democratic approaches to career education.* Lanham, MD: University Press of America.

Hyslop-Margison, E. J., & Graham, B. (2001). Principles for democratic learning in career education. *Canadian Journal of Education, 26*(3).

Orr, D. W. (2004). *Earth in mind: On education, environment, and the human prospect.* Washington, DC: Island Press.

Pinsky, R. (2002). *Democracy, culture and the voice of poetry.* Princeton, NJ: Princeton University Press.

Sears, A. M., & Hughes, A. S. (1996). Citizenship education and current educational reform. *Canadian Journal of Education, 21*(2).

YOUR KNOWLEDGE HAS VALUE

- We will publish your bachelor's and master's thesis, essays and papers

- Your own eBook and book - sold worldwide in all relevant shops

- Earn money with each sale

Upload your text at www.GRIN.com
and publish for free